TRADI NICARAGUAN COOKBOOK

AVA BAKER

TRADITIONAL NICARAGUAN COOKBOOK

Copyright © 2024 Ava Baker

All rights reserved.

CONTENTS

APPETIZERS AND SNACKS — 1

NACATAMALES — 1
QUESILLO (NICARAGUAN CHEESE TORTILLA) — 3
TOSTONES (FRIED GREEN PLANTAINS) — 5
YUCA FRITA CON CHICHARRÓN (FRIED CASSAVA WITH PORK) — 7
VIGORÓN (CABBAGE AND YUCA SALAD) — 8
GALLO PINTO EMPANADAS — 10
TAJADAS (FRIED SWEET PLANTAINS) — 12
TAMAL DE ELOTE (SWEET CORN TAMALE) — 13
BOLLOS DE MAZORCA (CORN TAMALES) — 15
QUESO FRITO (FRIED CHEESE) — 17

SOUPS AND STEWS — 18

SOPA DE MONDONGO (TRIPE SOUP) — 18
SOPA DE RES (BEEF SOUP) — 20
INDIO VIEJO (CHICKEN AND MAIZE STEW) — 22
SOPA DE ALBÓNDIGAS (MEATBALL SOUP) — 24
SOPA DE FRIJOLES (BEAN SOUP) — 26
SOPA DE LENTEJAS (LENTIL SOUP) — 28
SOPA DE CAMARONES (SHRIMP SOUP) — 30
SOPA DE GALLINA INDIA (GUINEA HEN SOUP) — 32
SOPA DE QUESO (CHEESE SOUP) — 34
SOPA DE CHAYOTE (CHAYOTE SQUASH SOUP) — 36

MAIN DISHES - MEAT — 38

BAHO (NICARAGUAN BEEF AND PLANTAIN STEW) — 38

Carne Asada (Grilled Meat)	40
Nica Pollo (Nicaraguan-Style Chicken)	42
Chancho con Yuca (Pork with Cassava)	44
Rondón (Coconut Seafood Stew)	46
Vigorón de Pescado (Fish Vigorón)	48
Gallina Rellena (Stuffed Chicken)	50
Fritanga (Mixed Fried Meats)	52
Costillas de Cerdo con Tamarindo (Pork Ribs with Tamarind)	54
Carne Deshilachada (Shredded Beef)	56

MAIN DISHES - VEGETARIAN 58

Ensalada de Repollo (Cabbage Salad)	58
Gallopinto con Plátanos Maduros (Mixed Rice and Beans with Ripe Plantains)	60
Yuca con Mojo (Cassava with Garlic Sauce)	62
Nacatamales Vegetarianos (Vegetarian Nacatamales)	64
Tostadas de Frijoles (Bean Tostadas)	67
Quesadilla Nica (Nicaraguan Sweet Cheese Bread)	69
Plátanos en Tentación (Sweet Glazed Plantains)	71
Arroz a la Valenciana (Valencian-Style Rice)	73
Pipián de Ayote (Squash Seed Sauce)	75
Nopales con Huevos (Cactus with Eggs)	77

DESSERTS 79

Tres Leches Cake	79
Rosquillas (Nicaraguan Donuts)	82
Atolillo de Elote (Corn Pudding)	84
Cajeta de Coco (Coconut Fudge)	86
Alfajores Nica (Nicaraguan Shortbread Cookies)	88
Leche Agria con Miel (Sour Milk with Honey)	90

QUESILLO DE MANGO (MANGO PUDDING)	92
BUÑUELOS (SWEET FRITTERS)	94
ARROZ CON LECHE (RICE PUDDING)	96
RIGUAS (NICARAGUAN CORN PANCAKES)	98
MEASURES	**100**

TRADITIONAL NICARAGUAN COOKBOOK

APPETIZERS AND SNACKS

Nacatamales

- Servings: 8-10
- Time: 4 hours (including preparation and cooking)

Ingredients:

- 3 cups masa harina
- 1 cup lard
- 1 cup chicken or pork broth
- 1 teaspoon baking powder
- 1 teaspoon salt
- 1 cup achiote oil
- 2 cups cooked and shredded pork
- 1 cup diced bell peppers

- 1 cup diced tomatoes
- 1 cup sliced onions
- 1 cup sliced green olives
- 1 cup raisins
- Banana leaves, softened in hot water

Directions:

1. In a large bowl, mix masa harina, lard, baking powder, and salt.
2. Gradually add broth and achiote oil, mixing until a smooth dough forms.
3. In a pan, sauté onions, bell peppers, and tomatoes until soft. Add shredded pork, olives, and raisins. Cook for an additional 5 minutes.
4. Spread masa on a softened banana leaf, add a spoonful of the pork mixture, and fold into a rectangular package.
5. Stack nacatamales in a large pot, add water, and steam for 3-4 hours.
6. Allow nacatamales to cool before serving.

Quesillo (Nicaraguan Cheese Tortilla)

- Servings: 6-8
- Time: 30 minutes

Ingredients:

- 2 cups masa harina
- 2 1/2 cups warm water
- 1 teaspoon salt
- 1 cup grated quesillo (Nicaraguan cheese)
- 1 cup thinly sliced onions, soaked in water
- Sour cream (optional)
- Pickled jalapeños (optional)

Directions:

1. In a bowl, combine masa harina, warm water, and salt to form a smooth dough.
2. Divide the dough into golf ball-sized portions and flatten each into a thin round tortilla.
3. On a hot griddle, cook the tortillas for 1-2 minutes on each side until they start to puff.
4. Sprinkle grated quesillo on each tortilla while still hot, allowing it to melt.

5. Add a handful of sliced onions to each tortilla, and optionally, top with sour cream and pickled jalapeños.
6. Fold the tortilla in half, creating a semi-circle shape.

Tostones (Fried Green Plantains)

- Servings: 4-6
- Time: 30 minutes

Ingredients:

- 4 green plantains, peeled and sliced into 1-inch thick rounds
- Vegetable oil for frying
- Salt to taste
- Mojo sauce (optional, for dipping)

Directions:

1. Heat vegetable oil in a deep pan over medium heat.
2. Fry plantain slices for 2-3 minutes on each side, or until they start to golden.
3. Remove from the oil and place on a paper towel to drain excess oil.
4. Using a tostonera or the bottom of a flat, heavy object, flatten each slice to about half its original thickness.
5. Return flattened plantains to the hot oil and fry for an additional 2-3 minutes on each side until crispy and golden.

6. Remove from the oil, sprinkle with salt, and place on a paper towel to absorb any remaining oil.
7. Serve immediately with mojo sauce for dipping.

Yuca Frita con Chicharrón (Fried Cassava with Pork)

- Servings: 4-6
- Time: 1 hour

Ingredients:

- 2 lbs yuca (cassava), peeled and cut into fries
- 1 lb pork belly, diced
- 2 cups vegetable oil (for frying)
- Salt to taste
- Lime wedges for serving

Directions:

1. Boil yuca in salted water until fork-tender, about 20-25 minutes. Drain and let it cool.
2. In a separate pan, fry diced pork belly until golden and crispy. Remove excess oil and set aside.
3. Heat vegetable oil in a deep pan to 350°F (175°C).
4. Fry boiled yuca in batches until golden brown, about 5-7 minutes per batch. Remove and drain on paper towels.
5. Season yuca with salt while hot and transfer to a serving plate.

6. Top yuca with crispy chicharrón (fried pork belly) and serve with lime wedges.

Vigorón (Cabbage and Yuca Salad)

- Servings: 4-6
- Time: 45 minutes

Ingredients:

- 1 large yuca (cassava), peeled and cut into bite-sized pieces
- 1 small cabbage, finely shredded
- 1 cup chicharrón (fried pork belly), diced
- 1 cup tomatoes, diced
- 1/2 cup red onion, thinly sliced
- 1/2 cup green bell pepper, thinly sliced
- 1/4 cup white vinegar
- Salt and pepper to taste

Directions:

1. Boil yuca in salted water until tender, about 15-20 minutes. Drain and let it cool.
2. In a large bowl, combine shredded cabbage, diced tomatoes, sliced red onion, and sliced green bell pepper.
3. Add the boiled yuca to the bowl, mixing gently with the vegetables.

4. In a separate bowl, dress the salad with white vinegar. Season with salt and pepper to taste.
5. Arrange the salad on a serving platter, topping it with diced chicharrón.

Gallo Pinto Empanadas

- Servings: 12-15 empanadas
- Time: 1 hour

Ingredients:

- 2 cups gallo pinto (cooked rice and beans)
- 1 cup cooked and shredded chicken
- 1 cup diced bell peppers
- 1/2 cup diced onions
- 1/4 cup chopped fresh cilantro
- 1 teaspoon ground cumin
- Salt and pepper to taste
- Empanada dough (store-bought or homemade)
- Vegetable oil for frying

Directions:

1. In a pan, sauté diced onions and bell peppers until softened.
2. Add shredded chicken, ground cumin, salt, and pepper. Cook until chicken is heated through.
3. In a large bowl, combine gallo pinto, the chicken mixture, and chopped cilantro. Mix well.
4. Roll out empanada dough and cut into rounds.

5. Place a spoonful of the gallo pinto mixture in the center of each dough round.
6. Fold the dough over the filling, creating a half-moon shape, and seal the edges by pressing with a fork.
7. Heat vegetable oil in a pan and fry empanadas until golden brown on both sides, about 3-4 minutes per side.
8. Drain excess oil on paper towels and serve.

Tajadas (Fried Sweet Plantains)

- Servings: 4-6
- Time: 20 minutes

Ingredients:

- 4 ripe plantains, peeled and sliced on a bias
- Vegetable oil for frying
- Salt to taste

Directions:

1. Heat vegetable oil in a pan over medium heat.
2. Fry plantain slices until golden brown on both sides, about 2-3 minutes per side.
3. Remove from the oil and place on a paper towel to absorb excess oil.
4. Using the back of a spoon, flatten each slice slightly.
5. Return the flattened plantains to the hot oil and fry for an additional 1-2 minutes per side until crispy.
6. Sprinkle with salt while hot and transfer to a serving plate.

Tamal de Elote (Sweet Corn Tamale)

- Servings: 8-10 tamales
- Time: 2 hours

Ingredients:

- 2 cups fresh corn kernels (from about 4 ears of corn)
- 1 cup corn masa harina
- 1/2 cup unsalted butter, softened
- 1/2 cup sugar
- 1/2 cup whole milk
- 1 teaspoon baking powder
- 1/2 teaspoon salt
- Corn husks, soaked in warm water

Directions:

1. In a blender, combine fresh corn kernels and milk. Blend until smooth.
2. In a large mixing bowl, beat together softened butter and sugar until creamy.
3. Add the corn masa harina, blended corn mixture, baking powder, and salt to the bowl. Mix well until a smooth batter forms.

4. Take a corn husk, spread a thin layer of the batter onto the center, and fold the sides to form a rectangular package. Tie with a strip of soaked husk.
5. Arrange tamales in a steamer, standing upright with open ends facing up.
6. Steam tamales for 1.5 to 2 hours or until the masa is firm and cooked through.
7. Allow tamales to cool for a few minutes before unwrapping.

Bollos de Mazorca (Corn Tamales)

- Servings: 8-10 tamales
- Time: 2 hours

Ingredients:

- 4 cups fresh corn kernels (from about 8 ears of corn)
- 1 cup corn masa harina
- 1/2 cup unsalted butter, melted
- 1/4 cup sugar
- 1/2 teaspoon salt
- Corn husks, soaked in warm water

Directions:

1. In a blender, puree half of the fresh corn kernels until smooth. Coarsely chop the remaining kernels.
2. In a large mixing bowl, combine the pureed corn, chopped corn, corn masa harina, melted butter, sugar, and salt. Mix well to form a thick batter.
3. Take a corn husk, spread a generous spoonful of the batter onto the center, and fold the sides to enclose the filling. Tie with a strip of soaked husk.
4. Arrange tamales in a steamer, standing upright with open ends facing up.

5. Steam tamales for about 1.5 to 2 hours or until the masa is set.
6. Allow tamales to cool for a few minutes before unwrapping.

Queso Frito (Fried Cheese)

- Servings: 4-6
- Time: 15 minutes

Ingredients:

- 1 lb firm cheese (such as queso fresco or panela), sliced into 1/2-inch thick rectangles
- 1 cup all-purpose flour
- 2 eggs, beaten
- Vegetable oil for frying
- Salt to taste

Directions:

1. Heat vegetable oil in a pan over medium heat.
2. Dredge each cheese slice in flour, ensuring even coating.
3. Dip the floured cheese into beaten eggs, covering it completely.
4. Fry the cheese slices in the hot oil until golden brown on both sides, about 2-3 minutes per side.
5. Remove from the oil and place on a paper towel to absorb excess oil.
6. Sprinkle with salt while hot and transfer to a serving plate.

TRADITIONAL NICARAGUAN COOKBOOK

SOUPS AND STEWS

Sopa de Mondongo (Tripe Soup)

- Servings: 6-8
- Time: 2 hours

Ingredients:

- 1 lb beef tripe, cleaned and diced
- 1 lb beef, cubed
- 1 large onion, finely chopped
- 2 bell peppers, diced
- 3 tomatoes, diced
- 3 cloves garlic, minced
- 1 cup carrots, sliced
- 1 cup potatoes, diced

- 1/2 cup celery, chopped
- 1/2 cup fresh cilantro, chopped
- 2 tablespoons vegetable oil
- Salt and pepper to taste

Directions:

1. In a large pot, boil the tripe until tender, about 1-1.5 hours. Drain and set aside.
2. In a separate pot, sauté onions, bell peppers, and garlic in vegetable oil until softened.
3. Add beef cubes and cook until browned on all sides.
4. Stir in tomatoes, carrots, potatoes, and celery. Cook for an additional 5 minutes.
5. Pour in enough water to cover the ingredients. Bring to a boil and then reduce heat to simmer.
6. Add the boiled tripe to the pot, season with salt and pepper, and simmer for another 30-40 minutes until flavors meld.
7. Just before serving, stir in fresh cilantro for a burst of flavor.

Sopa de Res (Beef Soup)

- Servings: 6-8
- Time: 2 hours

Ingredients:

- 1 lb beef stew meat, cubed
- 2 tablespoons vegetable oil
- 1 large onion, finely chopped
- 3 cloves garlic, minced
- 2 carrots, sliced
- 2 potatoes, diced
- 1 plantain, sliced
- 1/2 cup green beans, chopped
- 1/2 cup corn kernels
- 1/2 cup cabbage, shredded
- 2 tomatoes, diced
- 1/4 cup rice
- 8 cups beef broth
- Salt and pepper to taste
- Fresh cilantro for garnish

Directions:

1. In a large pot, heat vegetable oil over medium heat. Add beef stew meat and brown on all sides.
2. Add chopped onions and minced garlic, sautéing until aromatic and onions are translucent.
3. Pour in beef broth, bringing it to a boil. Reduce heat to a simmer.
4. Stir in carrots, potatoes, plantain, green beans, corn, cabbage, and tomatoes. Simmer for about 30 minutes.
5. Add rice to the pot, and continue to simmer until both rice and vegetables are tender, approximately 20-25 minutes.
6. Season with salt and pepper to taste.
7. Serve hot, garnished with fresh cilantro.

Indio Viejo (Chicken and Maize Stew)

- Servings: 6-8
- Time: 2 hours

Ingredients:

- 1 whole chicken, cut into pieces
- 2 cups maize dough (masa)
- 1 large onion, finely chopped
- 2 bell peppers, diced
- 3 tomatoes, diced
- 4 cloves garlic, minced
- 2 tablespoons achiote oil
- 1 cup sour orange juice (or a mix of orange and lime juice)
- 4 cups chicken broth
- 2 teaspoons dried oregano
- Salt and pepper to taste

Directions:

1. In a large pot, boil the chicken in chicken broth until fully cooked. Remove bones and shred the chicken.
2. In a separate pan, sauté onions, bell peppers, and garlic in achiote oil until softened.

3. Add diced tomatoes and continue cooking until tomatoes break down.
4. Stir in maize dough, mixing well to create a thick paste.
5. Combine the maize mixture with the shredded chicken in the pot.
6. Pour sour orange juice over the chicken and maize mixture, stirring continuously.
7. Season with oregano, salt, and pepper. Simmer for 30-40 minutes until flavors meld.

Sopa de Albóndigas (Meatball Soup)

- Servings: 4-6
- Time: 1 hour

Ingredients:

- 1 lb ground beef
- 1/2 cup rice, uncooked
- 1 egg
- 1/4 cup breadcrumbs
- 1/4 cup fresh cilantro, finely chopped
- 1/2 teaspoon cumin
- 1 teaspoon dried oregano
- 1 large carrot, sliced
- 1 cup green beans, cut into bite-sized pieces
- 1 cup corn kernels
- 1 large potato, diced
- 1/2 cup onions, finely chopped
- 3 cloves garlic, minced
- 8 cups beef or vegetable broth
- 2 tablespoons vegetable oil
- Salt and pepper to taste

Directions:

1. In a bowl, combine ground beef, rice, egg, breadcrumbs, cilantro, cumin, and oregano. Form into small meatballs.
2. In a pot, heat vegetable oil and sauté onions and garlic until softened.
3. Add meatballs to the pot and brown on all sides.
4. Pour in the broth and bring to a simmer.
5. Add carrots, green beans, corn, and potatoes to the pot. Cook until vegetables are tender.
6. Season with salt and pepper to taste.
7. Simmer for an additional 15-20 minutes, allowing flavors to meld.

Sopa de Frijoles (Bean Soup)

- Servings: 6-8
- Time: 1.5 hours

Ingredients:

- 2 cups black beans, soaked overnight
- 1 lb pork shoulder, diced
- 1 large onion, finely chopped
- 3 cloves garlic, minced
- 2 tomatoes, diced
- 1 bell pepper, diced
- 2 carrots, sliced
- 2 potatoes, diced
- 1/2 cup fresh cilantro, chopped
- 2 tablespoons vegetable oil
- 1 teaspoon ground cumin
- 1 teaspoon dried oregano
- Salt and pepper to taste

Directions:

1. Rinse soaked black beans and place them in a large pot. Cover with water and bring to a boil. Reduce heat and simmer until beans are tender, about 1 hour.

2. In a separate pan, heat vegetable oil and sauté onions and garlic until translucent.
3. Add diced pork to the pan and brown on all sides.
4. Stir in tomatoes, bell pepper, carrots, and potatoes. Cook for an additional 5 minutes.
5. Transfer the vegetable and pork mixture to the pot of simmering beans.
6. Season with ground cumin, dried oregano, salt, and pepper. Simmer for an additional 30 minutes.
7. Add fresh cilantro just before serving.

Sopa de Lentejas (Lentil Soup)

- Servings: 4-6
- Time: 1 hour

Ingredients:

- 1 cup dried lentils, rinsed
- 1 lb chorizo sausage, sliced
- 1 large onion, finely chopped
- 2 carrots, diced
- 2 potatoes, diced
- 3 cloves garlic, minced
- 1 bell pepper, diced
- 1 can (14 oz) diced tomatoes
- 6 cups chicken or vegetable broth
- 2 tablespoons olive oil
- 1 teaspoon ground cumin
- 1 teaspoon paprika
- Salt and pepper to taste
- Fresh parsley, chopped (for garnish)

Directions:

1. In a pot, heat olive oil and sauté onions and garlic until softened.

2. Add chorizo slices and cook until browned.
3. Stir in lentils, carrots, potatoes, bell pepper, ground cumin, and paprika. Cook for 5 minutes.
4. Pour in diced tomatoes and broth. Bring to a boil, then reduce heat and simmer until lentils are tender, about 30-40 minutes.
5. Season with salt and pepper to taste.
6. Serve the Sopa de Lentejas hot, garnished with fresh parsley.

Sopa de Camarones (Shrimp Soup)

- Servings: 4-6
- Time: 45 minutes

Ingredients:

- 1 lb large shrimp, peeled and deveined
- 1 large onion, finely chopped
- 3 cloves garlic, minced
- 2 tomatoes, diced
- 1 bell pepper, diced
- 1 carrot, sliced
- 1 potato, diced
- 6 cups fish or shrimp broth
- 1 cup coconut milk
- 2 tablespoons vegetable oil
- 1 teaspoon ground cumin
- 1 teaspoon paprika
- Salt and pepper to taste
- Fresh cilantro, chopped (for garnish)

Directions:

1. In a pot, heat vegetable oil and sauté onions and garlic until fragrant.

2. Add diced tomatoes, bell pepper, carrot, and potato. Cook for 5 minutes.
3. Stir in ground cumin and paprika, allowing the spices to meld with the vegetables.
4. Pour in fish or shrimp broth and bring to a simmer. Cook until vegetables are tender, about 20 minutes.
5. Add coconut milk to the pot, followed by the shrimp. Cook for an additional 5-7 minutes until shrimp are pink and cooked through.
6. Season with salt and pepper to taste.
7. Serve the Sopa de Camarones hot, garnished with fresh cilantro.

Sopa de Gallina India (Guinea Hen Soup)

- Servings: 6-8
- Time: 2.5 hours

Ingredients:

- 1 guinea hen, cleaned and cut into parts
- 1 large onion, finely chopped
- 3 cloves garlic, minced
- 2 tomatoes, diced
- 2 carrots, sliced
- 2 potatoes, diced
- 1 bell pepper, diced
- 1 plantain, peeled and sliced
- 1/2 cup rice
- 1/4 cup fresh cilantro, chopped
- 1 teaspoon ground cumin
- 1 teaspoon dried oregano
- Salt and pepper to taste

Directions:

1. In a large pot, bring the guinea hen to a boil in enough water to cover. Reduce heat and simmer until the meat is tender, about 1.5-2 hours.

2. In a separate pan, sauté onions and garlic until softened.
3. Add diced tomatoes, carrots, potatoes, bell pepper, and plantain to the pan. Cook for an additional 5 minutes.
4. Transfer the vegetable mixture to the pot with the guinea hen.
5. Stir in rice, ground cumin, and dried oregano. Cook until the rice is tender, about 20-25 minutes.
6. Season with salt and pepper to taste.
7. Just before serving, sprinkle fresh cilantro over the soup.

Sopa de Queso (Cheese Soup)

- Servings: 4-6
- Time: 30 minutes

Ingredients:

- 2 cups sharp cheddar cheese, grated
- 1 cup monterey jack cheese, grated
- 1/2 cup unsalted butter
- 1/2 cup all-purpose flour
- 4 cups whole milk
- 1 cup vegetable broth
- 1/2 cup onions, finely chopped
- 1/2 cup celery, finely chopped
- 1/2 cup carrots, finely chopped
- 3 cloves garlic, minced
- 1 teaspoon Dijon mustard
- Salt and pepper to taste
- Fresh chives, chopped (for garnish)

Directions:

1. In a pot, melt butter over medium heat. Add onions, celery, carrots, and garlic. Sauté until vegetables are tender.

2. Stir in flour to create a roux. Cook for 2-3 minutes, stirring constantly.
3. Gradually whisk in milk and vegetable broth, ensuring a smooth consistency.
4. Add Dijon mustard, salt, and pepper. Bring the mixture to a simmer.
5. Reduce heat to low and gradually add grated cheddar and monterey jack cheese, stirring until melted and creamy.
6. Simmer for an additional 10-15 minutes, allowing flavors to meld.
7. Adjust seasoning if needed.
8. Serve the Sopa de Queso hot, garnished with fresh chives.

Sopa de Chayote (Chayote Squash Soup)

- Servings: 4-6
- Time: 45 minutes

Ingredients:

- 3 chayote squash, peeled, seeded, and diced
- 1 large onion, finely chopped
- 2 carrots, sliced
- 2 potatoes, diced
- 3 cloves garlic, minced
- 1 teaspoon ground cumin
- 6 cups vegetable broth
- 1 cup milk
- 2 tablespoons vegetable oil
- Salt and pepper to taste
- Fresh cilantro, chopped (for garnish)

Directions:

1. In a pot, heat vegetable oil and sauté onions and garlic until fragrant.
2. Add diced chayote squash, carrots, and potatoes. Cook for 5 minutes.

3. Sprinkle ground cumin over the vegetables, stirring to coat evenly.
4. Pour in vegetable broth and bring to a simmer. Cook until the vegetables are tender, about 20-25 minutes.
5. Using a blender or immersion blender, puree the soup until smooth.
6. Return the soup to the pot, stir in milk, and bring back to a simmer.
7. Season with salt and pepper to taste.
8. Serve the Sopa de Chayote hot, garnished with fresh cilantro

MAIN DISHES - MEAT

Baho (Nicaraguan Beef and Plantain Stew)

- Servings: 6-8
- Time: 3 hours

Ingredients:

- 2 lbs beef shank or brisket, cut into chunks
- 4 green plantains, peeled and sliced
- 2 red onions, thinly sliced
- 4 cloves garlic, minced
- 2 tomatoes, diced
- 2 bell peppers, sliced
- 4 cups beef broth
- 2 cups orange juice

- 1 cup red wine
- 1/2 cup fresh cilantro, chopped
- 1/4 cup vegetable oil
- 2 teaspoons ground cumin
- 2 teaspoons dried oregano
- Salt and pepper to taste
- Banana leaves (for wrapping)

Directions:

1. In a large bowl, marinate beef chunks with minced garlic, ground cumin, dried oregano, salt, and pepper. Allow it to marinate for at least 30 minutes.
2. In a deep pot, heat vegetable oil over medium heat. Brown the marinated beef on all sides.
3. Add sliced onions, diced tomatoes, and bell peppers to the pot. Cook until vegetables are softened.
4. Pour in orange juice, red wine, and beef broth. Bring the mixture to a simmer.
5. Wrap the marinated beef and vegetable mixture in banana leaves, creating individual packages.
6. Place the wrapped packages back into the pot, covering them with additional banana leaves.
7. Simmer on low heat for 2-3 hours until the beef is tender and the flavors meld.

8. Garnish with chopped cilantro before serving.

Carne Asada (Grilled Meat)

- Servings: 4-6
- Time: 2 hours (including marination)

Ingredients:

- 2 lbs flank steak or skirt steak
- 1/4 cup orange juice
- 1/4 cup lime juice
- 4 cloves garlic, minced
- 1/4 cup fresh cilantro, chopped
- 2 teaspoons ground cumin
- 1 teaspoon paprika
- Salt and pepper to taste
- 1/4 cup vegetable oil

Directions:

1. In a bowl, mix together orange juice, lime juice, minced garlic, chopped cilantro, ground cumin, paprika, salt, and pepper to create the marinade.
2. Place the steak in a shallow dish and pour the marinade over it, ensuring the meat is well-coated. Marinate for at least 1-2 hours, or overnight for more flavor.
3. Preheat the grill to medium-high heat.

4. Remove the steak from the marinade and let excess liquid drip off.
5. Brush the steak with vegetable oil to prevent sticking to the grill.
6. Grill the steak for 4-5 minutes on each side, or until it reaches your desired level of doneness.
7. Let the carne asada rest for a few minutes before slicing it against the grain.
8. Serve the grilled meat with your favorite side dishes, tortillas, and salsa.

Nica Pollo (Nicaraguan-Style Chicken)

- Servings: 4-6
- Time: 1.5 hours

Ingredients:

- 1 whole chicken, cut into pieces
- 1/2 cup orange juice
- 1/4 cup lime juice
- 4 cloves garlic, minced
- 1 teaspoon ground cumin
- 1 teaspoon dried oregano
- 1 teaspoon paprika
- Salt and pepper to taste
- 1/4 cup vegetable oil
- 2 large onions, thinly sliced
- 2 bell peppers, sliced
- 2 tomatoes, diced
- 1 cup chicken broth
- 1/2 cup fresh cilantro, chopped (for garnish)

Directions:

1. In a bowl, combine orange juice, lime juice, minced garlic, ground cumin, dried oregano, paprika, salt, and pepper to create the marinade.
2. Place chicken pieces in a large dish and pour the marinade over them. Ensure each piece is well-coated. Marinate for at least 30 minutes.
3. In a large pan, heat vegetable oil over medium heat. Brown the marinated chicken on all sides.
4. Add sliced onions, bell peppers, and diced tomatoes to the pan. Cook until vegetables are softened.
5. Pour in chicken broth, cover the pan, and simmer for 45 minutes or until the chicken is fully cooked.
6. Garnish with chopped cilantro before serving.

Chancho con Yuca (Pork with Cassava)

- Servings: 4-6
- Time: 2 hours

Ingredients:

- 2 lbs pork shoulder, cut into chunks
- 2 lbs yuca (cassava), peeled and cut into chunks
- 2 large onions, finely chopped
- 4 cloves garlic, minced
- 2 tomatoes, diced
- 2 bell peppers, sliced
- 1/2 cup orange juice
- 1/4 cup lime juice
- 1 teaspoon ground cumin
- 1 teaspoon dried oregano
- Salt and pepper to taste
- 1/4 cup vegetable oil
- 1 cup chicken or pork broth
- 1/4 cup fresh cilantro, chopped (for garnish)

Directions:

1. In a bowl, mix orange juice, lime juice, minced garlic, ground cumin, dried oregano, salt, and pepper to create the marinade.
2. Marinate pork chunks in the mixture for at least 1 hour.
3. In a large pot, heat vegetable oil over medium heat. Brown the marinated pork on all sides.
4. Add chopped onions, bell peppers, and diced tomatoes to the pot. Cook until vegetables are softened.
5. Pour in chicken or pork broth and bring to a simmer. Cover and cook for 1 hour or until the pork is tender.
6. Add yuca chunks to the pot and continue cooking until both the pork and yuca are fully cooked and flavorful.
7. Garnish with chopped cilantro before serving.

Rondón (Coconut Seafood Stew)

- Servings: 4-6
- Time: 1.5 hours

Ingredients:

- 1 lb mixed seafood (shrimp, fish, calamari)
- 1 lb yuca (cassava), peeled and cut into chunks
- 1 lb sweet potatoes, peeled and diced
- 1 cup cherry tomatoes, halved
- 1 red onion, thinly sliced
- 1 bell pepper, sliced
- 3 cloves garlic, minced
- 2 tablespoons vegetable oil
- 2 cans (14 oz each) coconut milk
- 2 cups fish or seafood broth
- 1 teaspoon ground coriander
- 1 teaspoon ground cumin
- 1 teaspoon paprika
- Salt and pepper to taste
- Fresh cilantro, chopped (for garnish)

Directions:

1. In a large pot, heat vegetable oil over medium heat. Sauté sliced red onion and minced garlic until softened.
2. Add ground coriander, ground cumin, paprika, salt, and pepper. Stir to coat the onions and garlic with the spices.
3. Pour in coconut milk and fish or seafood broth. Bring to a simmer.
4. Add yuca chunks, sweet potatoes, and bell pepper slices to the pot. Cook until vegetables are tender.
5. Gently add mixed seafood and cherry tomatoes. Simmer until the seafood is cooked through.
6. Adjust seasoning if needed and let the flavors meld for an additional 10-15 minutes.
7. Garnish with chopped cilantro before serving.

Vigorón de Pescado (Fish Vigorón)

- Servings: 4-6
- Time: 1.5 hours

Ingredients:

- 1 lb white fish fillets (such as tilapia or snapper)
- 2 cups cabbage, shredded
- 2 cups yuca (cassava), boiled and cut into chunks
- 1 red onion, thinly sliced
- 3 tomatoes, diced
- 1 bell pepper, diced
- 3 cloves garlic, minced
- 1/4 cup fresh cilantro, chopped
- 1/4 cup orange juice
- 2 tablespoons vegetable oil
- Salt and pepper to taste

Directions:

1. Marinate fish fillets in orange juice, minced garlic, salt, and pepper. Let it marinate for at least 30 minutes.
2. In a pan, heat vegetable oil over medium heat. Cook the marinated fish fillets until they are fully cooked and flaky. Set aside.

3. In a large bowl, combine shredded cabbage, boiled yuca chunks, sliced red onion, diced tomatoes, and diced bell pepper.
4. Place the cooked fish fillets on top of the cabbage and yuca mixture.
5. Drizzle with additional orange juice and sprinkle chopped cilantro over the top.

Gallina Rellena (Stuffed Chicken)

- Servings: 4-6
- Time: 2 hours

Ingredients:

- 1 whole chicken (about 4 lbs)
- 1 cup rice, cooked
- 1/2 lb ground pork
- 1/2 cup raisins
- 1/4 cup almonds, chopped
- 1/4 cup green olives, sliced
- 2 tomatoes, diced
- 1 bell pepper, diced
- 1 large onion, finely chopped
- 4 cloves garlic, minced
- 1/4 cup vegetable oil
- 1 teaspoon ground cumin
- 1 teaspoon dried oregano
- Salt and pepper to taste
- Toothpicks or kitchen twine (for securing)

Directions:

1. Preheat the oven to 375°F (190°C).

2. In a pan, heat vegetable oil over medium heat. Sauté onions and garlic until softened.
3. Add ground pork and cook until browned. Stir in diced tomatoes, diced bell pepper, ground cumin, dried oregano, salt, and pepper. Cook for an additional 5 minutes.
4. In a bowl, combine cooked rice, raisins, chopped almonds, and sliced green olives. Mix well.
5. Stuff the chicken cavity with the rice mixture and the prepared pork mixture.
6. Secure the stuffed chicken with toothpicks or kitchen twine to hold the filling in place.
7. Place the stuffed chicken in a roasting pan, and roast in the preheated oven for about 1.5 to 2 hours, or until the chicken is cooked through and golden brown.
8. Let the Gallina Rellena rest for a few minutes before carving.

Fritanga (Mixed Fried Meats)

- Servings: 4-6
- Time: 1.5 hours

Ingredients:

- 1 lb pork belly, sliced
- 1 lb beef sirloin, sliced
- 1 lb chorizo sausage, sliced
- 1 lb morcilla (blood sausage), sliced
- 2 cups yuca (cassava), boiled and cut into chunks
- 2 cups green plantains, sliced
- 1 cup cabbage, shredded
- 1 cup tomatoes, diced
- 1 cup onions, thinly sliced
- 4 cloves garlic, minced
- 1/4 cup vegetable oil
- 2 teaspoons ground cumin
- Salt and pepper to taste
- Fresh cilantro, chopped (for garnish)

Directions:

1. In a large frying pan, heat vegetable oil over medium heat.

2. Fry pork belly slices until crispy. Remove and set aside.
3. In the same pan, fry beef sirloin slices until browned. Remove and set aside.
4. Fry chorizo and morcilla slices until cooked through. Remove and set aside.
5. In the remaining oil, fry boiled yuca and green plantains until golden brown and crispy. Remove and set aside.
6. In the same pan, sauté sliced onions and minced garlic until softened.
7. Add shredded cabbage, diced tomatoes, ground cumin, salt, and pepper. Cook until vegetables are tender.
8. Arrange all the fried meats, yuca, and green plantains on a serving platter.
9. Garnish with the sautéed vegetables and fresh cilantro.

Costillas de Cerdo con Tamarindo (Pork Ribs with Tamarind)

- Servings: 4-6
- Time: 2.5 hours

Ingredients:

- 2 lbs pork ribs
- 1 cup tamarind pulp
- 1/2 cup brown sugar
- 1/4 cup soy sauce
- 2 tablespoons vegetable oil
- 1 large onion, finely chopped
- 4 cloves garlic, minced
- 1 teaspoon ground cumin
- 1 teaspoon paprika
- Salt and pepper to taste
- Fresh cilantro, chopped (for garnish)

Directions:

1. Preheat the oven to 325°F (163°C).
2. In a bowl, mix tamarind pulp, brown sugar, soy sauce, ground cumin, paprika, salt, and pepper to create the marinade.

3. Place the pork ribs in a shallow dish and pour the marinade over them. Ensure each rib is well-coated. Marinate for at least 1-2 hours, or overnight for more flavor.
4. In a large oven-safe pan, heat vegetable oil over medium heat. Sauté chopped onions and minced garlic until softened.
5. Add the marinated pork ribs to the pan, searing them on all sides.
6. Transfer the pan to the preheated oven and roast for about 2 hours, basting the ribs with the marinade occasionally until they are tender.
7. Garnish with chopped cilantro before serving.

Carne Deshilachada (Shredded Beef)

- Servings: 4-6
- Time: 3 hours

Ingredients:

- 2 lbs beef chuck roast
- 1 large onion, chopped
- 4 cloves garlic, minced
- 2 tomatoes, diced
- 1 bell pepper, sliced
- 2 bay leaves
- 1 teaspoon ground cumin
- 1 teaspoon dried oregano
- Salt and pepper to taste
- 4 cups beef broth
- 2 tablespoons vegetable oil

Directions:

1. In a large pot, heat vegetable oil over medium heat. Sear the beef chuck roast on all sides until browned.
2. Add chopped onions, minced garlic, and sliced bell pepper to the pot. Cook until the vegetables are softened.

3. Stir in diced tomatoes, ground cumin, dried oregano, salt, and pepper. Cook for an additional 5 minutes.
4. Pour in beef broth and add bay leaves. Bring to a simmer.
5. Cover the pot and simmer on low heat for about 2.5 to 3 hours or until the beef is tender and easily shreds.
6. Once the beef is cooked, shred it using two forks.
7. Continue simmering the shredded beef in the pot for an additional 30 minutes, allowing it to absorb the flavors.
8. Adjust seasoning if needed before serving.

MAIN DISHES - VEGETARIAN

Ensalada de Repollo (Cabbage Salad)

- Servings: 4-6
- Time: 15 minutes

Ingredients:

- 1/2 head green cabbage, finely shredded
- 1 carrot, grated
- 1/2 red onion, thinly sliced
- 1/4 cup fresh cilantro, chopped
- 1/4 cup mayonnaise
- 2 tablespoons white vinegar
- 1 teaspoon sugar
- Salt and pepper to taste

Directions:

1. In a large bowl, combine shredded green cabbage, grated carrot, thinly sliced red onion, and chopped cilantro.
2. In a small bowl, whisk together mayonnaise, white vinegar, sugar, salt, and pepper to create the dressing.
3. Pour the dressing over the cabbage mixture and toss until well coated.
4. Adjust salt and pepper to taste.
5. Chill in the refrigerator for at least 30 minutes before serving to allow the flavors to meld.

Gallopinto con Plátanos Maduros (Mixed Rice and Beans with Ripe Plantains)

- Servings: 4-6
- Time: 30 minutes

Ingredients:

- 2 cups cooked white rice, chilled
- 1 cup black beans, cooked and drained
- 2 ripe plantains, sliced
- 1 large onion, finely chopped
- 2 cloves garlic, minced
- 1 red bell pepper, diced
- 1/4 cup fresh cilantro, chopped
- 2 tablespoons vegetable oil
- 1 teaspoon ground cumin
- Salt and pepper to taste

Directions:

1. In a large pan, heat vegetable oil over medium heat. Sauté chopped onions and minced garlic until softened.
2. Add diced red bell pepper and sliced ripe plantains to the pan. Cook until plantains are golden brown on both sides.

3. Stir in cooked black beans and ground cumin. Cook for an additional 3-5 minutes.
4. Add chilled cooked white rice to the pan, mixing it with the plantain and bean mixture.
5. Season with salt and pepper to taste.
6. Continue cooking, stirring occasionally, until the gallopinto is heated through.
7. Garnish with chopped cilantro before serving.

Yuca con Mojo (Cassava with Garlic Sauce)

- Servings: 4-6
- Time: 45 minutes

Ingredients:

- 2 lbs yuca (cassava), peeled and cut into chunks
- 4 cloves garlic, minced
- 1/2 cup extra-virgin olive oil
- 2 tablespoons fresh lime juice
- 1 teaspoon dried oregano
- Salt to taste
- Fresh parsley, chopped (for garnish)

Directions:

1. Place yuca chunks in a pot of salted water and bring to a boil. Reduce heat and simmer until the yuca is fork-tender, about 20-25 minutes.
2. While the yuca is cooking, prepare the mojo sauce. In a small saucepan, heat olive oil over medium heat. Add minced garlic and sauté until golden but not browned.
3. Remove the saucepan from heat and stir in fresh lime juice, dried oregano, and salt. Set aside.

4. Once the yuca is cooked, drain it and arrange the yuca chunks on a serving platter.
5. Pour the prepared mojo sauce over the yuca.
6. Garnish with chopped fresh parsley before serving.

Nacatamales Vegetarianos (Vegetarian Nacatamales)

- Servings: 8-10
- Time: 4 hours

Ingredients:

For the Dough:

- 4 cups masa harina
- 2 cups vegetable broth
- 1 cup vegetable oil
- 1 teaspoon baking powder
- Salt to taste

For the Filling:

- 2 cups cooked black beans, mashed
- 2 cups cooked rice
- 2 cups butternut squash, diced
- 1 cup bell peppers, diced
- 1 cup tomatoes, diced
- 1 cup green peas
- 1/2 cup fresh cilantro, chopped
- 1/4 cup green olives, sliced
- 2 tablespoons vegetable oil

- 2 tablespoons achiote paste
- 2 teaspoons ground cumin
- 2 teaspoons dried oregano
- Salt and pepper to taste

For Assembly:

- Banana leaves (cut into 8-10 inch squares)
- Cooking twine or banana leaf strips

Directions:

1. Prepare the Banana Leaves:
   - Soften banana leaves by briefly passing them over an open flame or soaking them in warm water.
2. Make the Dough:
   - In a large bowl, combine masa harina, vegetable broth, vegetable oil, baking powder, and salt. Mix until you achieve a soft, spreadable consistency.
3. Prepare the Filling:
   - In a pan, heat vegetable oil over medium heat. Add achiote paste, ground cumin, dried oregano, and sauté briefly.
   - Add diced butternut squash, bell peppers, tomatoes, and green peas. Cook until vegetables are tender.

- Stir in mashed black beans, cooked rice, chopped cilantro, and sliced green olives. Cook for an additional 5 minutes. Season with salt and pepper.

4. Assemble the Nacatamales:
- Place a banana leaf square on a clean surface.
- Spread a portion of the masa dough onto the center of the banana leaf, forming a rectangle.
- Spoon a generous amount of the vegetable filling onto the masa dough.
- Fold the banana leaf over the filling, then fold the sides to create a rectangular packet. Secure with cooking twine or banana leaf strips.

5. Steam the Nacatamales:
- Arrange the assembled nacatamales in a steamer, stacking them if necessary.
- Steam for approximately 2-3 hours or until the masa is cooked and has a firm consistency.

6. Serve:
- Carefully unwrap the banana leaves and serve the Vegetarian Nacatamales hot.

Tostadas de Frijoles (Bean Tostadas)

- Servings: 4-6
- Time: 20 minutes

Ingredients:

- 1 can (15 oz) black beans, drained and rinsed
- 2 cloves garlic, minced
- 1 teaspoon ground cumin
- 1 teaspoon chili powder
- Salt and pepper to taste
- 2 tablespoons vegetable oil
- 8 tostada shells
- 1 cup lettuce, shredded
- 1 cup tomatoes, diced
- 1/2 cup queso fresco, crumbled
- 1/4 cup fresh cilantro, chopped (for garnish)
- Sour cream (optional, for serving)

Directions:

1. In a pan, heat vegetable oil over medium heat. Add minced garlic and sauté until fragrant.

2. Add drained black beans, ground cumin, chili powder, salt, and pepper to the pan. Cook for about 5 minutes, mashing the beans slightly with the back of a spoon.
3. Meanwhile, warm the tostada shells in the oven according to package instructions.
4. Spread the seasoned black beans evenly over each tostada shell.
5. Top with shredded lettuce, diced tomatoes, and crumbled queso fresco.
6. Garnish with chopped cilantro.
7. Optional: Add a dollop of sour cream on top.

Quesadilla Nica (Nicaraguan Sweet Cheese Bread)

- Servings: 8-10
- Time: 1 hour

Ingredients:

- 2 cups all-purpose flour
- 1 cup sugar
- 1 teaspoon baking powder
- 1/2 teaspoon salt
- 1 cup unsalted butter, softened
- 4 large eggs
- 1 teaspoon vanilla extract
- 1 cup queso fresco, crumbled
- 1 cup mozzarella cheese, shredded
- 1/2 cup whole milk

Directions:

1. Preheat the oven to 350°F (175°C). Grease and flour a baking dish.
2. In a bowl, whisk together the flour, baking powder, and salt.

3. In a separate large bowl, cream together the softened butter and sugar until light and fluffy.
4. Add the eggs one at a time, beating well after each addition. Stir in the vanilla extract.
5. Gradually add the dry ingredients to the wet ingredients, mixing until just combined.
6. Fold in the crumbled queso fresco, shredded mozzarella, and whole milk until the batter is smooth.
7. Pour the batter into the prepared baking dish, spreading it evenly.
8. Bake for 40-45 minutes or until the top is golden brown and a toothpick inserted into the center comes out clean.
9. Allow the Quesadilla Nica to cool before slicing.

Plátanos en Tentación (Sweet Glazed Plantains)

- Servings: 4-6
- Time: 20 minutes

Ingredients:

- 4 ripe plantains, peeled and sliced
- 1/2 cup brown sugar
- 1/4 cup unsalted butter
- 1/4 cup water
- 1 teaspoon ground cinnamon
- 1/4 teaspoon ground cloves
- 1/4 teaspoon salt
- 1/4 cup raisins (optional)
- 1/4 cup chopped nuts (such as walnuts or pecans), toasted (optional)
- Vanilla ice cream (optional, for serving)

Directions:

1. In a skillet, melt the unsalted butter over medium heat.
2. Add sliced plantains to the skillet and cook until golden brown on both sides.

3. Sprinkle brown sugar over the plantains, stirring gently to coat them evenly.
4. Pour water over the plantains and add ground cinnamon, ground cloves, and salt. Stir to combine.
5. Reduce heat to low and simmer for about 10-12 minutes, allowing the plantains to absorb the flavors and the sauce to thicken.
6. Optional: Stir in raisins for added sweetness and texture.
7. Optional: Toast chopped nuts in a separate pan and sprinkle them over the glazed plantains.
8. Serve the Plátanos en Tentación warm, either on their own or with a scoop of vanilla ice cream.

Arroz a la Valenciana (Valencian-Style Rice)

- Servings: 4-6
- Time: 45 minutes

Ingredients:

- 2 cups medium-grain rice
- 1/2 lb chicken, cut into pieces
- 1/2 lb pork, diced
- 1/2 lb rabbit or chorizo sausage, sliced
- 1/2 cup green beans, chopped
- 1/2 cup lima beans
- 1 red bell pepper, diced
- 1 tomato, diced
- 1 onion, finely chopped
- 3 cloves garlic, minced
- 4 cups chicken broth
- 1/2 teaspoon saffron threads
- 1/2 teaspoon smoked paprika
- 1/4 cup olive oil
- Salt and pepper to taste
- Lemon wedges (for serving)

Directions:

1. In a small bowl, steep saffron threads in a couple of tablespoons of warm water for 10 minutes.
2. In a large paella pan or skillet, heat olive oil over medium heat. Add chicken, pork, and rabbit or chorizo. Brown the meat on all sides.
3. Add chopped onion and minced garlic to the pan. Sauté until the onions are translucent.
4. Stir in diced tomatoes and diced red bell pepper. Cook until the vegetables are softened.
5. Add green beans, lima beans, smoked paprika, salt, and pepper to the pan. Mix well.
6. Pour in rice and sauté for a couple of minutes until the rice is coated with the mixture.
7. Add chicken broth and the saffron-infused water to the pan. Bring to a simmer.
8. Reduce heat to low and cook uncovered for about 20-25 minutes or until the rice is cooked and the liquid is absorbed.
9. Optional: Place the paella pan in the oven for the last 5-10 minutes to develop a crispy layer at the bottom of the rice (socarrat).
10. Let the Arroz a la Valenciana rest for a few minutes before serving.
11. Serve with lemon wedges on the side.

Pipián de Ayote (Squash Seed Sauce)

- Servings: 4-6
- Time: 30 minutes

Ingredients:

- 1 cup raw squash seeds (pepitas)
- 2 cups diced ayote (squash)
- 2 tomatoes, diced
- 1 onion, chopped
- 2 cloves garlic, minced
- 2 cups vegetable or chicken broth
- 2 tablespoons vegetable oil
- 1 teaspoon ground cumin
- 1 teaspoon dried oregano
- 1/2 teaspoon chili powder (optional, for heat)
- Salt and pepper to taste
- Fresh cilantro, chopped (for garnish)

Directions:

1. In a dry pan, toast raw squash seeds (pepitas) over medium heat until they become golden and fragrant. Set aside a small portion for garnish.

2. In the same pan, heat vegetable oil over medium heat. Add chopped onion and minced garlic, sautéing until softened.
3. Add diced ayote (squash) to the pan and cook until it begins to soften.
4. Stir in diced tomatoes and continue cooking until they release their juices.
5. Add toasted squash seeds, ground cumin, dried oregano, chili powder (if using), salt, and pepper. Mix well.
6. Pour in vegetable or chicken broth and bring the mixture to a simmer. Cook for an additional 10-15 minutes until the squash is tender.
7. Using a blender or immersion blender, puree the mixture until smooth.
8. Adjust seasoning if needed and garnish with chopped cilantro and the reserved toasted squash seeds before serving.
9. Serve the Pipián de Ayote as a flavorful sauce over rice, vegetables, or your favorite protein.

Nopales con Huevos (Cactus with Eggs)

- Servings: 2-4
- Time: 20 minutes

Ingredients:

- 1 cup nopales (cactus paddles), cleaned and diced
- 4 eggs
- 1 tomato, diced
- 1/2 onion, finely chopped
- 2 cloves garlic, minced
- 2 tablespoons vegetable oil
- 1 jalapeño, seeded and diced (optional, for heat)
- Salt and pepper to taste
- Fresh cilantro, chopped (for garnish)

Directions:

1. If using fresh nopales, clean them thoroughly, removing spines and nodes. Dice the nopales into small pieces.
2. In a pan, heat vegetable oil over medium heat. Add chopped onion and minced garlic, sautéing until softened.
3. Add diced nopales to the pan and cook until they become tender.

4. Stir in diced tomatoes and jalapeño (if using). Cook until the tomatoes release their juices.
5. Create wells in the nopales mixture and crack the eggs into the wells.
6. Season the eggs with salt and pepper.
7. Cover the pan and cook until the eggs are cooked to your liking.
8. Optional: For a quicker egg cooking process, you can also whisk the eggs before pouring them into the wells, creating a scrambled egg and nopales mixture.
9. Garnish with chopped cilantro before serving.

DESSERTS

Tres Leches Cake

- Servings: 12
- Time: 1 hour

Ingredients:

- 1 cup all-purpose flour
- 1 1/2 teaspoons baking powder
- 1/4 teaspoon salt
- 1/2 cup unsalted butter, softened
- 1 cup granulated sugar
- 4 large eggs
- 1 teaspoon vanilla extract
- 1/2 cup whole milk

Tres Leches Mixture:

- 1 can (14 oz) sweetened condensed milk
- 1 can (12 oz) evaporated milk
- 1 cup whole milk

Whipped Cream Topping:

- 1 cup heavy cream
- 2 tablespoons powdered sugar
- 1 teaspoon vanilla extract

Directions:

1. Preheat the oven to 350°F (175°C). Grease and flour a 9x13-inch baking pan.
2. In a bowl, whisk together the flour, baking powder, and salt.
3. In a separate large bowl, cream together the softened butter and sugar until light and fluffy.
4. Add the eggs one at a time, beating well after each addition. Stir in the vanilla extract.
5. Gradually add the dry ingredients to the wet ingredients, mixing until just combined.
6. Stir in the 1/2 cup of whole milk until the batter is smooth.

7. Pour the batter into the prepared baking pan and spread it evenly.
8. Bake for 25-30 minutes or until a toothpick inserted into the center comes out clean.
9. While the cake is baking, prepare the tres leches mixture by combining the sweetened condensed milk, evaporated milk, and 1 cup of whole milk in a bowl.
10. Once the cake is out of the oven, poke holes all over the surface using a fork or skewer.
11. Pour the tres leches mixture evenly over the warm cake, allowing it to absorb the liquid.
12. Allow the cake to cool completely in the refrigerator.
13. For the whipped cream topping, beat the heavy cream, powdered sugar, and vanilla extract until stiff peaks form.
14. Spread the whipped cream over the chilled cake.
15. Optional: Garnish with a sprinkle of cinnamon or a dusting of cocoa powder.

Rosquillas (Nicaraguan Donuts)

- Servings: 12-16 donuts
- Time: 1.5 hours

Ingredients:

- 3 cups all-purpose flour
- 1 tablespoon baking powder
- 1/2 teaspoon salt
- 1/2 cup unsalted butter, softened
- 1 cup granulated sugar
- 2 large eggs
- 1 teaspoon vanilla extract
- 1/2 cup milk
- Vegetable oil (for frying)

Glaze:

- 2 cups powdered sugar
- 1/4 cup milk
- 1 teaspoon vanilla extract

Directions:

1. In a bowl, whisk together the flour, baking powder, and salt.

2. In a separate large bowl, cream together the softened butter and sugar until light and fluffy.
3. Add the eggs one at a time, beating well after each addition. Stir in the vanilla extract.
4. Gradually add the dry ingredients to the wet ingredients, alternating with the milk, beginning and ending with the dry ingredients. Mix until just combined.
5. Cover the dough and refrigerate for at least 1 hour.
6. On a floured surface, roll out the chilled dough to a 1/2-inch thickness.
7. Use a round cookie cutter or a glass to cut out donut shapes. Use a smaller round cutter or the cap of a bottle to cut out the center of each donut.
8. In a deep pan, heat vegetable oil to 350°F (175°C).
9. Carefully place the donuts into the hot oil, frying until they are golden brown on both sides. Ensure they are cooked through by testing one donut first.
10. Remove the donuts from the oil and place them on paper towels to absorb excess oil.
11. In a bowl, whisk together the powdered sugar, milk, and vanilla extract to create the glaze.
12. Dip each donut into the glaze, ensuring they are coated evenly.
13. Allow the glaze to set for a few minutes before serving.

Atolillo de Elote (Corn Pudding)

- Servings: 6-8
- Time: 45 minutes

Ingredients:

- 2 cups fresh or frozen corn kernels
- 2 cups whole milk
- 1/2 cup cornmeal
- 1/2 cup sugar
- 1/4 teaspoon ground cinnamon
- Pinch of salt
- 1 teaspoon vanilla extract
- Cinnamon sticks (for garnish)

Directions:

1. In a blender, combine corn kernels and 1 cup of milk. Blend until smooth.
2. In a bowl, whisk together cornmeal and the remaining 1 cup of milk until well combined.
3. In a saucepan, combine the corn puree, cornmeal mixture, sugar, ground cinnamon, and a pinch of salt.

4. Cook the mixture over medium heat, stirring constantly to avoid lumps, until it thickens to a pudding-like consistency (about 15-20 minutes).
5. Once the mixture has thickened, remove it from heat and stir in the vanilla extract.
6. Pour the Atolillo de Elote into serving bowls or cups.
7. Garnish each serving with a cinnamon stick.

Cajeta de Coco (Coconut Fudge)

- Servings: 12-16 pieces
- Time: 1 hour

Ingredients:

- 2 cups shredded coconut
- 1 can (14 oz) sweetened condensed milk
- 1 cup granulated sugar
- 1/2 cup unsalted butter
- 1/4 cup water
- 1 teaspoon vanilla extract
- Pinch of salt

Directions:

1. In a dry pan, toast the shredded coconut over medium heat until it becomes golden and fragrant. Set aside a small portion for topping.
2. In a saucepan, combine sweetened condensed milk, granulated sugar, unsalted butter, water, and a pinch of salt.
3. Cook the mixture over medium-low heat, stirring constantly, until the sugar dissolves and the mixture thickens (about 30-40 minutes).

4. Stir in the toasted shredded coconut and continue cooking for an additional 10-15 minutes, or until the fudge reaches a soft ball stage (when a small amount dropped into cold water forms a soft ball).
5. Remove the saucepan from heat and stir in vanilla extract.
6. Pour the coconut fudge mixture into a greased or lined square baking dish.
7. Sprinkle the reserved toasted coconut over the top.
8. Allow the Cajeta de Coco to cool and set at room temperature or in the refrigerator before cutting it into squares.

Alfajores Nica (Nicaraguan Shortbread Cookies)

- Servings: 24-30 cookies
- Time: 1.5 hours

Ingredients:

For the Cookies:

- 2 cups all-purpose flour
- 1 cup cornstarch
- 1 cup unsalted butter, softened
- 1/2 cup powdered sugar
- 1 teaspoon vanilla extract
- Pinch of salt

For the Filling:

- 1 cup dulce de leche

For the Coating:

- 1 cup powdered sugar

Directions:

1. Preheat the oven to 350°F (175°C). Line a baking sheet with parchment paper.
2. In a bowl, whisk together the all-purpose flour and cornstarch.
3. In a separate large bowl, cream together the softened butter and powdered sugar until light and fluffy.
4. Add the vanilla extract and a pinch of salt to the butter mixture. Mix well.
5. Gradually add the dry ingredients to the wet ingredients, mixing until a soft dough forms.
6. Roll out the dough on a floured surface to about 1/4 inch thickness.
7. Use a round cookie cutter to cut out individual cookies. Place them on the prepared baking sheet.
8. Bake for 10-12 minutes or until the edges are just beginning to turn golden.
9. Allow the cookies to cool completely on a wire rack.
10. Once cooled, spread a layer of dulce de leche on the bottom side of one cookie and sandwich it with another.
11. Roll the edges of the cookie sandwich in powdered sugar to coat.
12. Repeat the process with the remaining cookies.

Leche Agria con Miel (Sour Milk with Honey)

- Servings: 2
- Time: 5 minutes (plus fermentation time)

Ingredients:

- 2 cups whole milk
- 2 tablespoons plain yogurt with live active cultures
- 2 tablespoons honey (adjust to taste)

Directions:

1. Heat the whole milk in a saucepan until it is warm but not boiling. Allow it to cool to a temperature where it is comfortable to touch.
2. In a glass or ceramic container, combine the warm milk with the plain yogurt, stirring well to mix.
3. Cover the container with a clean cloth or plastic wrap and place it in a warm, draft-free area to ferment. Allow it to sit for 6-12 hours, or until it thickens and develops a tangy flavor.
4. Once the milk has soured to your liking, refrigerate it to slow down the fermentation process.

5. When ready to serve, drizzle honey over the Leche Agria, adjusting the amount to your desired sweetness.
6. Stir the honey into the sour milk and serve chilled.

Quesillo de Mango (Mango Pudding)

- Servings: 4-6
- Time: 2 hours (including chilling time)

Ingredients:

- 3 ripe mangoes, peeled, pitted, and diced
- 1 can (14 oz) sweetened condensed milk
- 1 cup whole milk
- 1/4 cup cornstarch
- 1 teaspoon vanilla extract
- Pinch of salt
- Fresh mint leaves (for garnish)

Directions:

1. In a blender, puree the diced mangoes until smooth.
2. In a bowl, whisk together the sweetened condensed milk, whole milk, cornstarch, vanilla extract, and a pinch of salt until well combined.
3. Pour the milk mixture into a saucepan and heat over medium heat, stirring constantly until it thickens into a custard-like consistency (about 10-15 minutes).
4. Remove the saucepan from heat and allow the milk mixture to cool slightly.

5. Gradually whisk the mango puree into the milk mixture until smooth and well incorporated.
6. Pour the mango pudding into individual serving bowls or glasses.
7. Refrigerate for at least 1-2 hours, or until the pudding is set.
8. Garnish with fresh mint leaves before serving.

Buñuelos (Sweet Fritters)

- Servings: 12-16 fritters
- Time: 1.5 hours

Ingredients:

For the Dough:

- 2 cups all-purpose flour
- 2 teaspoons baking powder
- 1/4 teaspoon salt
- 1/2 cup sugar
- 1/4 cup unsalted butter, melted
- 2/3 cup whole milk
- 2 large eggs
- 1 teaspoon vanilla extract
- Vegetable oil (for frying)

For the Coating:

- 1/2 cup granulated sugar
- 1 teaspoon ground cinnamon

Directions:

1. In a bowl, whisk together the all-purpose flour, baking powder, and salt.

2. In a separate large bowl, combine sugar and melted butter. Mix until well incorporated.
3. Add eggs, one at a time, to the sugar and butter mixture. Stir in the vanilla extract.
4. Gradually add the dry ingredients to the wet ingredients, alternating with the whole milk, beginning and ending with the dry ingredients. Mix until just combined.
5. Cover the dough and let it rest for 30 minutes.
6. In a deep pan, heat vegetable oil over medium heat to 350°F (175°C).
7. Drop spoonfuls of dough into the hot oil, frying until golden brown on both sides. Ensure they are cooked through by testing one fritter first.
8. Remove the fritters from the oil and place them on paper towels to absorb excess oil.
9. In a shallow bowl, mix granulated sugar and ground cinnamon for the coating.
10. While the fritters are still warm, roll them in the cinnamon sugar mixture to coat evenly.

Arroz con Leche (Rice Pudding)

- Servings: 6-8
- Time: 1.5 hours

Ingredients:

- 1 cup white rice
- 4 cups whole milk
- 1 cinnamon stick
- 1 cup sugar
- 1 teaspoon vanilla extract
- 1/2 cup raisins (optional)
- Ground cinnamon (for garnish)

Directions:

1. Rinse the white rice under cold water until the water runs clear.
2. In a saucepan, combine the rice, whole milk, and cinnamon stick. Bring to a boil, then reduce the heat to low and simmer, stirring occasionally, until the rice is tender and the mixture thickens (about 25-30 minutes).
3. Add sugar and continue cooking over low heat, stirring constantly, until the sugar is dissolved.
4. If using raisins, stir them into the rice pudding.

5. Remove the cinnamon stick and discard it.
6. Stir in vanilla extract and continue cooking for an additional 10-15 minutes, or until the rice pudding reaches your desired consistency.
7. Remove the saucepan from heat and let the rice pudding cool to room temperature.
8. Refrigerate for at least 1 hour before serving.
9. Serve the Arroz con Leche chilled, garnished with a sprinkle of ground cinnamon.

Riguas (Nicaraguan Corn Pancakes)

- Servings: 8-10 pancakes
- Time: 1 hour

Ingredients:

- 2 cups fresh corn kernels (from about 4 ears of corn)
- 1 cup masa harina (corn flour)
- 1/2 cup all-purpose flour
- 1 cup milk
- 2 tablespoons unsalted butter, melted
- 1 teaspoon baking powder
- 1 teaspoon salt
- Vegetable oil (for cooking)
- Queso fresco, crumbled (for serving)
- Sour cream (for serving)

Directions:

1. In a blender, combine fresh corn kernels and milk. Blend until smooth.
2. In a large mixing bowl, combine the corn and milk mixture with masa harina, all-purpose flour, melted butter, baking powder, and salt. Mix until well combined.

3. Allow the batter to rest for 15-20 minutes to let the masa harina hydrate.
4. Heat a skillet or griddle over medium heat and lightly coat with vegetable oil.
5. Pour 1/4 cup of batter onto the hot griddle for each pancake.
6. Cook the riguas until the edges are set and small bubbles form on the surface, then flip and cook the other side until golden brown.
7. Repeat the process until all the batter is used, adding more oil to the griddle as needed.
8. Serve the riguas warm, topped with crumbled queso fresco and a dollop of sour cream.

MEASURES

1. Volume Conversions:
   - 1 cup = 240 milliliters
   - 1 tablespoon = 15 milliliters
   - 1 teaspoon = 5 milliliters
   - 1 fluid ounce = 30 milliliters
2. Weight Conversions:
   - 1 ounce = 28 grams
   - 1 pound = 453 grams
   - 1 kilogram = 2.2 pounds
3. Temperature Conversions:
   - Celsius to Fahrenheit: $F = (C \times 9/5) + 32$
   - Fahrenheit to Celsius: $C = (F - 32) \times 5/9$
4. Length Conversions:
   - 1 inch = 2.54 centimeters

- 1 foot = 30.48 centimeters
- 1 meter = 39.37 inches

5. **Common Ingredient Conversions:**
   - 1 stick of butter = 1/2 cup = 113 grams
   - 1 cup of flour = 120 grams
   - 1 cup of sugar = 200 grams

6. **Oven Temperature Conversions:**
   - Gas Mark 1 = 275°F = 140°C
   - Gas Mark 2 = 300°F = 150°C
   - Gas Mark 4 = 350°F = 180°C
   - Gas Mark 6 = 400°F = 200°C
   - Gas Mark 8 = 450°F = 230°C.

Made in the USA
Columbia, SC
17 May 2025